Mix & Match MAMA

Kids IN THE KITCHEN

SHAY SHULL

HARVEST HOUSE PUBLISHERS
EUGENE, OREGON

Kids in the Kitchen

Copyright © 2017 Mix and Match Mama
Published by Harvest House Publishers
Eugene, Oregon 97402
www.harvesthousepublishers.com

ISBN 978-0-7369-6896-6 (soft cover)
ISBN 978-0-7369-6897-3 (eBook)

Cover by Nicole Dougherty
Interior design by Faceout Studio
Food photography by Shay Shull
All other photos by Jay Eads
Published in association with William K. Jensen Literary Agency, 119 Bampton
Court, Eugene, Oregon 97404.

Printed in China

16 17 18 19 20 21 22 23 24 25 / DS – FO / 10 9 8 7 6 5 4 3 2 1

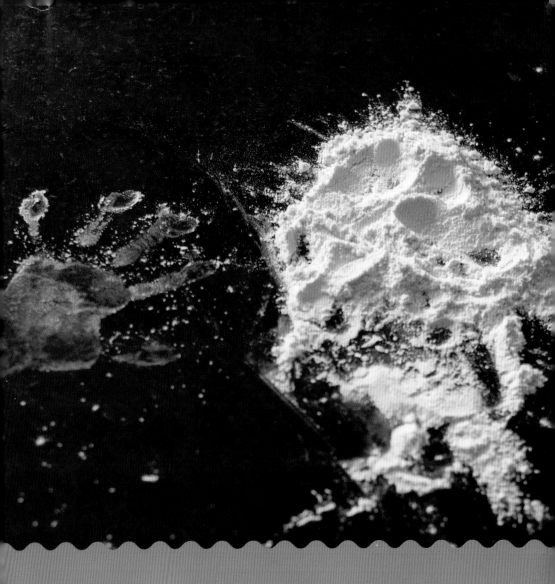

To Kensington, Smith, Ashby, and Madeley.
I'm so thankful that I get to be your mom.

xo

Contents

INTRODUCTION

Kids in the kitchen. Sounds like such a great idea, right? You and your children standing by the sink, stirring, chopping, tasting, and laughing. So innocent. So sweet. So not happening that way at my house. I'm a mom of four kiddos, and when we're all in the kitchen together, it's total chaos. Flour on the floor, pushing and shoving over who gets to hold the electric hand mixer, eggs being cracked at the wrong time, shells in the batter, loud talking, fast talking, so much talking… wildness in the kitchen. And I love every messy minute.

When my kids look back on their childhood, I want it to be filled with memories of all of us in the kitchen together. I want them to grow up and know how to make a cake, brown ground beef, stir risotto, and press a panini. I want them to have pride and confidence in the kitchen and to be familiar with all sorts of ingredients. I want them to have the same passion in their soul their mama does for food and family.

This isn't one of those cookbooks that teaches you how to sneak veggies into everything your kids eat. (Those books are great—this just isn't one of them.) This is one of those books where you turn pages, pick out fun, kid-friendly recipes the whole family will love, and work together as a little team to make them. My goal always is for you to spend less time cooking and more time with your family…so it's a bonus when that time cooking (though brief!) includes your kids. From my crazy, kid-filled kitchen to yours, have fun and enjoy. The days are long but the years are short. This sweet time will be gone in a flash, so we'd better soak up every moment.

Tips and Tricks

Kids are much more able in the kitchen than you might think. Believe it or not, my kiddos can do everything from perfectly crack an egg to brown a pound of ground beef. Sure, it took some practice—and lots of patience! But because we all try to have a good attitude (and…let's face it…I have a handheld vacuum), we successfully navigate our way through recipes every day. Here are some of my favorite tips and tricks for every age.

Birth to Age Two

- When my kiddos were babies, I would pull them up to the kitchen counter, hand them a rubber spatula to bang around, and just let them watch me cook in the kitchen. As I worked, I talked to them about the names of the foods we were using, pointed out the bright colors and different shapes, and had them feel the various textures. Even when they were too young to talk, I made sure to tell them a lot about food and show them how much fun cooking was.

- Tasting is such a big key to cooking with kids! No matter what I prepared, I always had some spoons on hand to let them (safely) taste the ingredients. As they watch you cook, they taste…and they learn.

Toddlers and Preschoolers

- Plastic knives and soft foods are so great for toddlers and preschoolers in the kitchen! I give my kiddos a plastic knife (so they won't cut themselves) and then something soft to cut (like bread, bananas, or avocados). Super simple—and they feel totally involved in the food prep.

- My kids learned a phrase that I still say over and over again: "Low and slow." I let my toddlers and preschoolers start out by stirring stuff in our mixing bowls, reminding them to stir *low* and *slow*. (Keep the spoon low in the bowl, and stir slowly to avoid spilling.)

- Pouring is perfect for kids this age! I measure out the ingredients—both liquid and dry—and let the kiddos pour away. Sure, sometimes spills happen, but they wipe up quickly, and the little ones are having so much fun that it's totally worth the mess.

Elementary Ages

- My kiddos can crack an egg better than some adults! And you know how they learned? Lots of practice! I let my kids practice cracking eggs over an empty bowl just for the experience. My rule of thumb? *Use your thumbs.* Crack the egg on the hard side of your bowl and then use your thumbs to break away the shell. After some practice, my kids could crack eggs into the bowl without any shell getting inside. Practice makes perfect when it comes to eggs!

- The "low and slow" rule comes into play with beaters too! My kids know how to attach the beaters to the electric mixer and mix together ingredients. Keeping things low and slow avoids spilling. Kids are fascinated by how the ingredients change as they all get mixed together. Super simple entertainment—and super fun!

- Kids this age can brown meat too. At first, I started by showing them how I brown a pound of ground beef. That's right—low and slow, which prevents grease spattering. After they watched me do it, they practiced stirring once the meat was nearly browned. Soon enough, they were browning it themselves from start to finish.

EGG-CELLENT
BREAKFASTS

Eggs are the perfect thing to make with and for kids. They're great for break-fast, easy for lunch, and delicious for dinner too. Egg recipes are typically really simple and can be made in advance. Plus, when you cook with eggs, you give your kiddos the opportunity to practice cracking. You'll be amazed at how well your kids can learn to crack an egg with just a few tries. I just don't think a busy mom can have enough egg recipes in her repertoire.

Breakfast Pizza with Biscuits
Eggs-tremely Delicious Breakfast Cups
Bacon and Avocado Scrambled Eggs over Waffles
Sausage Crescent Breakfast Casserole
Spinach and Chorizo Breakfast Casserole

Breakfast Pizza with Biscuits

Sometimes my kids just need a little pizza with their breakfast. We use canned biscuits for our crust and then build our little pizzas right on top. Since we're talking breakfast, we'll add some chopped bacon along with pepperoni and pizza sauce. After these guys bake in the oven, my kids love topping them with a fried egg and some chives. Sometimes we even make this little breakfast gem at suppertime too.

This recipe makes eight little pizzas.

INGREDIENTS

1 (16-ounce) can biscuits

1 (14-ounce) bottle pizza sauce

8 slices uncooked bacon, chopped

About 1 cup sliced pepperoni

About 1½ cups mozzarella cheese, shredded

8 eggs

Chopped chives to garnish

Preheat the oven to 400 degrees.

Grease a baking sheet or cover it with parchment paper. Open the can of biscuits, spread out each one with your fingers just a little bit, and place it on the baking sheet. Spoon a little pizza sauce on top of each biscuit.

Next, sprinkle the chopped bacon, a few pepperoni slices, and some cheese on each pizza.

Pop the pizzas into the oven and bake 8 to 10 minutes or until the edges are golden brown.

While the pizzas are baking, fry (or even scramble!) the eggs in a large skillet over medium heat.

Once the pizzas are ready, remove them from the oven, top with an egg and a sprinkle of chives, and breakfast (or dinner) is served!

Eggs-tremely Delicious Breakfast Cups

These little egg cups are simple to whip up. We like to pop them in the freezer and then in the morning, pull out as many as we like, microwave for 30 seconds, and *bam*...our family is fed! We love chopped turkey bacon and green onions, but you can mix and match whatever you love—browned sausage, turkey, pepperoni, and any combination of veggies you like. Bonus: You can omit the meat and veggies altogether and just keep this a simple egg and cheese cup. Kids will love these!

This recipe makes 12 breakfast cups.

INGREDIENTS

12 eggs, lightly beaten

About 6 to 8 slices cooked bacon, crumbled

About 4 green onions, chopped

½ cup cheese, shredded

Preheat the oven to 350 degrees.

Line a 12-cup muffin tin with muffin liners. In a large bowl, combine the eggs, bacon, green onions, and cheese. Fill each muffin cup ⅔ full with the mixture. Bake 25 minutes. Remove from the oven and cool about 5 minutes before removing the cups from the muffin tin. Serve immediately or freeze.

Bacon and Avocado Scrambled Eggs over Waffles

There's a little taco joint not too far from where we live that serves *the best* bacon and avocado tacos, so...we turned that into an egg breakfast and put it on top of a waffle. A meal that can be eaten any time of day, and so perfect for cooking with kids! My kiddos and I made these for brunch one day and they were a HUGE hit! Kids love putting everything on the waffle. Yep, it's a waffle...with scrambled eggs, bacon, and avocado on top. Amen.

This recipe serves four.

INGREDIENTS

1 dozen eggs

3 splashes milk or half-and-half

Salt and pepper

8 pieces crispy bacon, roughly chopped

2 avocados, halved, seeded, and cut into chunks

About 10 green onions, chopped

1 cup Pepper Jack (or Monterey Jack) cheese, shredded

4 fluffy waffles
(I just whipped some up with Bisquick!)

In a large mixing bowl, scramble the eggs with a whisk. Whisk in the milk along with a nice pinch of both salt and pepper.

Lightly coat a skillet with cooking spray, and scramble the eggs with a spatula over medium-high heat. After about a minute, stir in the bacon pieces, avocado chunks, green onions, and cheese.

Serve each person one waffle with a big scoop of scrambled eggs on top. Garnish with a few more chopped green onions.

The waffle adds a nice carb to this protein meal, but you could totally omit it if you like.

Eggs are my oldest daughter's favorite things to eat, so I'm always looking for new and inventive ways to prepare them. Eggs are great because they're inexpensive, readily available, and easily doubled to serve a crowd. They're a hit any time of day or night.

Sausage Crescent Breakfast Casserole

This recipe is a winner. Everyone loves it, and it's always gone within minutes. This dish is great for busy Sunday mornings before you head out to church. You can prepare it the night before and pop it in the oven the next day. Your family will be happy and full on their way out the door! Plus, there are lots of steps your kiddos can help with—pressing down the crescent roll dough, browning the sausage, whisking the eggs, and sprinkling on the cheese. Fun to make…better to make together!

This recipe serves about six to eight.

INGREDIENTS

1 can crescent rolls

1 pound pork breakfast sausage

6 eggs

½ cup milk

1 (4-ounce) can chopped green chilies

Salt and pepper

1½ cups Cheddar cheese, shredded

Preheat the oven to 350 degrees. Spread the crescent roll dough across the bottom of a greased (I use Pam) 9 x 13 baking dish. Make sure to press down on the seams so that the dough completely covers the dish. Set it aside.

Brown the sausage in a skillet over medium-high heat until it's browned and crumbly.

Meanwhile, whisk the eggs in a small bowl with the milk, chopped green chilies, and a good pinch of salt and pepper. Once the sausage is browned, spread it over the crescent roll layer in the pan. Pour the egg mixture on top of the sausage and sprinkle the cheese on top of that.

At this point, you can cover and refrigerate until you're ready to cook it the next morning, or you can go ahead and pop it in the oven for 25 to 30 minutes. The edges will be brown and the center not wobbly when it's done.

Spinach and Chorizo Breakfast Casserole

Letting kids try new flavors is always such fun! Chorizo is a great example. It's a Spanish pork sausage with a little kick, but it's not too spicy for kids…it's flavorful. You can substitute any pork sausage if you can't find chorizo. Shredded hash brown potatoes, spicy sausage, a little cheese, spinach, and egg all baked together? Yum-my!

This recipe serves about six to eight.

INGREDIENTS

1 (1-pound) chorizo sausage (or any pork sausage)

4 cups frozen shredded hash browns (lightly thawed but do not have to be thawed all the way)

6 eggs, beaten

2 cups milk

1 (10-ounce) package frozen spinach, thawed and all excess water squeezed out

2 cups Monterey Jack cheese, shredded and divided

Salt and pepper

Preheat the oven to 350 degrees. Grease (I use Pam) a 9 x 13 baking dish. Set it aside.

Brown the sausage over medium-high heat until it's cooked through and crumbled. (If your sausage comes in a casing, remove it from the casing to brown.) Meanwhile, combine the eggs, milk, spinach, and 1 cup of cheese in a bowl along with a big pinch of salt and pepper.

Layer the cooked sausage across the bottom of your prepared baking dish and then sprinkle the hash browns on top. Next, pour the egg mixture over the top. Finally, top with the remaining cup of cheese.

Bake the casserole uncovered for 45 to 50 minutes.

Remove from the oven, let set a few minutes, and then slice into squares and serve.

MONKEYS, MUFFINS,
AND OTHER
MORNING MEALS

One of the first things my kids learned to bake with me were muffins and breads. Kids learn measuring, stirring, counting, and pouring with all of these recipes. And there is instant gratification when making a muffin or sweet bread...it can be had as a snack! No waiting for dessert time to devour these sweet treats.

Chocolate Banana Muffins
Pineapple Muffins
Pumpkin Chocolate Chip Muffins
Ham, Bacon, and Gruyère Pinwheels
Snickerdoodle Monkey Bread
Simple Cinnamon Rolls
Whole Wheat Banana Butterscotch Waffles

Chocolate Banana Muffins

My kiddos love these muffins as after-school snacks, as breakfast, or as dessert at night. They're just good...every single time! The fun part? You can *mix and match* this recipe. Instead of chocolate, you could use a spice cake mix or yellow cake mix. And the fun part of making these muffins? Using the blender! Kids love it. So easy. So delicious. So fun to make together!

This recipe yields one dozen muffins.

INGREDIENTS

1 egg

¼ cup butter, softened

1 cup mashed bananas (about 1 ½ bananas)

1 box chocolate cake mix

1 cup chocolate chips

Preheat the oven to 350 degrees.

Line a 12-cup muffin tin with muffin liners. Set it aside.

Put the egg, butter, and mashed bananas in a blender. Blend until smooth. Pour the blender ingredients into a bowl, and then stir in the cake mix and chocolate chips. The batter will be nice and thick. Divide the batter evenly among the muffin cups.

Bake about 18 minutes or until a toothpick inserted into the center of a muffin comes out clean.

Remove from the oven and enjoy.

☀ **Hint:** These muffins freeze beautifully too! Place them in a freezer bag, and then pop them out and microwave for 30 seconds for an after-school snack.

Pineapple Muffins

My kiddos love it when we make three-ingredient pumpkin muffins, but when they requested them in *May*, I just wasn't feeling the pumpkin. So we substituted crushed pineapple for the pumpkin and...the perfect spring and summer muffin was born. Bonus: This recipe has only two ingredients—yellow cake mix and a can of crushed pineapple. It's perfect for busy families!

This recipe should make about 18 muffins.

INGREDIENTS

1 box yellow cake mix
1 (15-ounce) can crushed pineapple, undrained

Preheat the oven to 350 degrees.

Put paper muffin liners in 2 12-cup muffin tins.

In a mixing bowl, combine the two ingredients with an electric mixer. Pour the batter into each muffin liner (filling ¾ of the way full).

Bake about 12 to 15 minutes or until a toothpick inserted into the center comes out clean.

Remove from the oven and serve warm or at room temperature.

Pumpkin Chocolate Chip Muffins

These little muffins are always a huge hit with my kids! I love them because they're so simple and my kids love them because they're delish. Turn your kiddos lose with the ingredients, and these will be the easiest muffins you ever make!

This recipe makes one dozen muffins.

INGREDIENTS

1 box yellow cake mix

1 tablespoon cinnamon

1 (15-ounce) can of pumpkin (I use Libby's)

1 cup chocolate chips

Preheat the oven to 350 degrees.

Line a 12-cup muffin tin with muffin liners.

In a mixing bowl, combine the cake mix and cinnamon with the canned pumpkin and work it with a spoon. The batter will be pretty thick. Once the ingredients are combined, stir in the chocolate chips.

Fill the muffin liners ⅔ of the way full and bake about 15 minutes.

Remove from the oven and let cool in the pan 5 minutes before removing.

☀ **Tip:** You can swap the yellow cake mix and cinnamon for a box of spice cake mix instead!

Ham, Bacon, and Gruyère Pinwheels

These yummy little bites are always favorites with my kids. They're great for appetizers or quick little breakfast bites. I've even served them for lunch. I'm telling you, *everyone* loves these little pinwheels. Ham. Bacon. Gruyère. I mean...how could they *not* be good?

This recipe makes about 14 pinwheels.

INGREDIENTS

1 (17-ounce) box puff pastry sheets (from the freezer department—I use Pepperidge Farm)

8 slices really great ham
(I use Boar's Head Sun Dried Tomato Ham)

8 slices Gruyère cheese

8 slices uncooked bacon

Preheat the oven to 400 degrees.

Line a baking sheet with foil and lightly spray with Pam. Set it aside.

Make sure the puff pastry sheets are at room temperature, per box directions.

On the counter, open and lay out both puff pastry sheets. Next, lay four slices of ham down the center of each one. Next, top the ham with four slices of Gruyère down the center. Finally, lay four pieces of uncooked bacon down the center of each puff pastry sheet.

Roll the puff pastry sheet into a log starting with the left side, continuing across the middle (where your filling is) and all the way to the right side. Your puff pastry should now be in a log. Press the seam down to make sure it doesn't come apart.

Slice each log into about 7 pieces and then lay each pinwheel piece flat on your prepped baking sheet. Bake the pinwheels about 8 to 10 minutes. Remove from the oven and serve immediately.

Snickerdoodle Monkey Bread

We are monkey bread people. It's simple to make, it pairs perfectly with coffee (or chocolate milk), and it just makes a weekend morning feel a little more special. My kids and I have made a chocolate version, a butterscotch version, an eggnog version, and now a *snickerdoodle* version...because when you find a good method, you should just *mix and match* it. The perfect family fall breakfast—cinnamon-y goodness...right here!

INGREDIENTS

½ cup sugar

2 tablespoons cinnamon, divided

2 (16.3-ounce) cans refrigerated biscuit dough, cut into quarters (I use Pillsbury Grands)

¾ cup firmly packed brown sugar

½ cup butter

¼ cup light corn syrup

1 small (3.4-ounce) box instant vanilla pudding mix, dry and not prepared

Preheat the oven to 350 degrees.

Spray a Bundt pan with Pam. (Spray it well!)

In a small bowl, combine the sugar and 1 tablespoon of cinnamon. Dredge the biscuit quarters in the sugar mixture to coat them. Layer them in the prepared pan.

(At this point, you could cover your pan and pop it in the fridge until the next morning.)

In a small saucepan, combine the remaining tablespoon of cinnamon, brown sugar, butter, corn syrup, and instant pudding mix. Cook over medium-high heat, stirring constantly until the mixture comes to a boil. Boil for 1 minute. Pour over the layered biscuits.

Bake 35 to 40 minutes or until lightly browned. Invert immediately onto a platter and serve warm.

Simple Cinnamon Rolls

The other morning, we decided to make some really simple cinnamon rolls for our lazy Saturday. And I mean to tell you, these are super simple! If you have a can of biscuits on hand, you can whip 'em up in no time.

This recipe yields 14 to 16 super simple cinnamon rolls.

INGREDIENTS

2 (16-ounce) cans refrigerated biscuit dough (I use Pillsbury Grands)

½ cup butter, softened

About 2 cups pecan pieces

About 3 tablespoons cinnamon

1 (8-ounce) package cream cheese, softened

2 cups powdered sugar

About 1 tablespoon milk

Preheat the oven to 350 degrees.

Grease (I use Pam) a pie plate. Set it aside.

Slightly roll out each biscuit on the counter. (Or you can just press it out a little bit with your fingers.) Spread about half a tablespoon of butter on each biscuit and add a few pecan pieces and a sprinkle of cinnamon. Roll the biscuit into a log and place it inside your pie plate. Repeat until you've squeezed all the biscuits into the pie plate. (I fit 14 in mine.)

Pop the pie plate into the oven and bake for about 10 minutes or until the biscuits are lightly browned.

Meanwhile, make your icing. Using an electric mixer, beat the cream cheese, powdered sugar, and milk. Add a little more sugar if your icing is too thin or more milk if it's too thick. Set the icing aside.

When the biscuits are ready, pull them from the oven and immediately spread the cream cheese icing over the top. Serve warm.

Whole Wheat Banana Butterscotch Waffles

Two kid favorites—bananas and butterscotch—in a family favorite waffle. The bananas make these waffles extra moist, and the whole wheat flour makes Mama feel less guilty about adding the butterscotch chips. You can make big waffles or small waffles...whatever your family likes best. And once you drizzle maple syrup on top...*yum.* Your kiddos will flip over these guys!

This recipe will yield enough batter for four big Belgian waffles or eight smaller waffles.

INGREDIENTS

2 cups whole wheat flour

2 teaspoons baking powder

Salt

2 tablespoons sugar

1 cup milk

1 egg, lightly beaten

2 bananas, mashed

1 cup butterscotch chips

Maple syrup for drizzling

Preheat the waffle iron. Lightly coat the surface with cooking spray.

In a large mixing bowl, combine the flour, baking powder, salt, and sugar with a whisk. In a second large mixing bowl, combine the milk, egg, and mashed bananas.

Slowly whisk the wet ingredients into the dry ingredients. Combine but do not overmix. Once everything is combined, stir in the butterscotch chips.

Ladle the batter into a hot waffle iron and bake to your liking.

Remove and serve with your favorite maple syrup.

Baking breakfast recipes with my kids is one of our favorite Saturday morning traditions. We sleep in, we gather around the counter, we stir, we mix, we add, we taste, we get excited about our morning meal. And it's always way more fun when that meal includes some of our favorite flavors, like butterscotch!

SUPER SNACKS
AND SIDES

I get asked all the time what snacks I make for my kids. Sometimes it's a home-made goodie, and other times it's a granola bar right out of the box. That's life, right? However, my kids always think it's so fun when I have a yummy (and homemade!) snack waiting for them after school. Whether it's warm (like my applesauce) or cold (like my popsicles), they get excited. Some of these snacks and sides are savory, some are sweet, and they're all delicious.

No-Bake Peanut Butter Bites

Autumn Applesauce

Green Machine Protein Smoothie

Roasted Everything

Sweet Pea Hummus

Poppin' Chickpeas

Greek Yogurt Popsicles

Peanut Butter Chocolate
Chip Popsicles

Toasted Coconut Cream Popsicles

No-Bake Peanut Butter Bites

Your kids can practically make these little balls of happiness on their own. They're sure to please your crew at snack time, breakfast time, or even for dessert. For our family, the key is to tuck just a few little butterscotch chips inside…and we like to eat them frozen. (Straight out of the freezer, they're gone in seconds!) A glass of milk is the perfect accompaniment to this deliciousness.

This recipe makes a dozen balls.

INGREDIENTS

1 cup creamy peanut butter

1½ cups old-fashioned oatmeal
(even quick-cooking oatmeal works!)

½ cup butterscotch chips

In a mixing bowl, combine the peanut butter, oatmeal, and butterscotch chips. Roll into balls and place on a plate. When you're done rolling, pop these yummy balls into the freezer for at least an hour (up to a week). Remove and enjoy cold.

Autumn Applesauce

The kids and I love to make applesauce on Sunday afternoons. Not only does it make our house smell delicious, it makes our dinner a little extra special too. If you have a slow cooker, this little method is a cinch to make (and the leftovers keep in your fridge up to three days!). Enjoy it as a snack, a side, a breakfast dish, or an ingredient in something else…just enjoy it.

This makes about four cups of applesauce.

INGREDIENTS

8 apples, peeled, cored, and sliced into chunks (I use Honeycrisp but Gala or McIntosh work well too)

1 cup water

½ cup light brown sugar

1½ tablespoons cinnamon

In your slow cooker, combine all 4 ingredients and then cover and cook on low for 7 to 8 hours or on high for 4 hours.

Remove the lid from the slow cooker and use a hand mixer to lightly mix the ingredients until they resemble the consistency you like. (I like my applesauce a little chunky.) You could also pour the ingredients into a food processor and pulse until you reach your desired consistency.

Serve warm or cold.

Green Machine Protein Smoothie

We're all about the smoothies in our house. Besides our coffeemaker, our blender does the most heavy lifting in the kitchen.

This recipe makes two kid-sized smoothies or one large smoothie.

INGREDIENTS

½ frozen banana

½ scoop vanilla protein powder

1 Granny Smith apple, cored but not peeled

2 cups fresh baby spinach (sounds like a lot but it will turn into nothing!)

1 cup ice

1 cup coconut milk

Add all the ingredients into your blender. Once everything is blended, serve and enjoy right away. If your blender isn't moving quickly, you might need to add a titch more liquid (either more coconut milk or water).

I've found several keys to getting kids to drink smoothies (even ones secretly filled with veggies!):

- Make the **color really vivid**. Nothing turns off a kid more than a brown or murky-looking smoothie. If you want your kids to eat spinach, add only bright green or clear ingredients to the blender (don't throw in a carrot). Bright, clear colors are so much more appealing.

- I like to **add a half scoop of vanilla protein powder** to my kids' smoothies on occasion. Yummy vanilla goes great with just about everything…or if you want a dark, chocolaty-rich smoothie, add a half scoop of chocolate protein powder (peanut butter and spinach pair nicely with it!).

- **Add lots of ice!** Smoothies are so much better when they're cold. I put at least a cup of ice in the blender.

- **Adding coconut milk or almond milk** is a great way to make your kids' smoothies rich but dairy-free.

- **Have frozen bananas ready to go.** We buy bananas, peel them, halve them, and then freeze them in a storage bag. Then, when we're ready to make our smoothies, we just pop out one frozen banana half and go. Bananas stay good so much longer when they're frozen.

Roasted Everything

One of my very favorite sides is roasted vegetables. For the most part, I don't enjoy eating veggies raw, but if you roast them? I can't eat enough! Roasting veggies for your family as a side dish is one of the simplest things you can do. You can roast fresh veggies or frozen, you can roast them whether they're in season or not (turn a bland, out-of-season tomato into something spectacular by roasting it), and you can mix and match and roast several varieties at one time. Next time you need a side, just roast it!

Some veggies need to roast longer than others. Broccoli, cauliflower, green beans, potatoes, and such need to roast 45 minutes to an hour, while cherry tomatoes, peas, and asparagus only need about 15 minutes. Your nose will know when it's time to pull them out...they'll just smell roasted up and delicious.

This go-to method is as simple as spreading out your veggies onto a foil-lined baking sheet (for easy cleanup) and then drizzling them with a healthy dose of olive oil, followed by a very generous pinch of salt and pepper. (The kiddos can do these steps!) Pop them in your preheated oven (I like 425 degrees) and let the roasting begin. About halfway through the cooking time, open the oven door and flip everything around a bit. It's as simple as that.

For an extra kick of flavor, let the kids squeeze some lemon over the top once the veggies are out and ready to be served...or a sprinkle of Parmesan too.

Sweet Pea Hummus

Don't think your kids will eat hummus? Think again! My Sweet Pea Hummus is sure to please even the pickiest of palates. (Don't call it hummus...call it dip!) And it's super fun to make...kids love seeing the ingredients change consistency in the food processor. Want to make it even more kid-friendly? Give them goldfish crackers for dunking. *Winning.*

INGREDIENTS

2 garlic cloves, chopped

2 (15-ounce) cans chickpeas, rinsed and drained

2 cups frozen or fresh peas

About ¼ cup extra virgin olive oil

Salt and pepper

Put the chopped garlic in a food processor and zip it around a few times. Next, add the peas (they can be frozen) and chickpeas. With the food processor set on puree, slowly drizzle the olive oil through the top of the food processor while pulsing the mixture. Stop and scrape the sides once or twice. Once the hummus reaches the desired consistency, remove the lid and stir in a healthy pinch of both salt and pepper. Enjoy right away or refrigerate up to two weeks.

Poppin' Chickpeas

I'm kind of obsessed with chickpeas…I could eat an entire batch all by myself in one sitting! And the first key to getting my kids to snack on chickpeas is, don't tell them they're called chickpeas. The minute they hear the word *peas*, they're out. I call them *poppers*. The second key to getting my kiddos to eat chickpeas (which are full of protein, by the way!) is to make them flavorful. Sorry…guess you might have to share after all.

Here's my method for the best roasted chickpeas. If you want to flavor yours differently, just omit the olive oil, salt, and pepper and add your favorite seasonings. One can of chickpeas… endless possibilities.

INGREDIENTS

1 (15-ounce) can chickpeas, rinsed and drained

Salt and pepper

Extra virgin olive oil

Preheat the oven to 425 degrees.

Line a baking sheet with foil for easy cleanup. Pour the rinsed and drained chickpeas right onto your baking sheet and spread them out. Drizzle on a tablespoon or so of olive oil and a good pinch of both salt and pepper. Pop these guys in the oven and roast about 25 minutes.

Remove from the oven and either serve immediately or store in an airtight container. They can be eaten warm, at room temperature, or even cold. Your kids will love poppin' these guys! (Just don't tell them they're chickpeas!)

Chickpeas are one of my family's very favorite things to snack on. You can roast them up simply or you can add your favorite seasonings and flavors. Here are some of my family's top picks:

- a tablespoon of chili powder (they'll taste like a taco)

- a tablespoon or so of grated Parmesan cheese

- half a tablespoon of sugar with a pinch of cinnamon (yes…they can be sweet too!)

- a bit of garlic powder

- a little lemon zest

Let your imagination run wild with these little poppers. Before you know it, you and your kids will be poppin' them in your mouths left and right!

Greek Yogurt Popsicles

During the summer, my kiddos become popsicle-obsessed…like, to the point where we whip up these fun frozen treats *daily*. My kids love the rich taste of these Greek yogurt creations, and I love that they're getting a little protein too. What a fun frozen treat…so creamy and flavorful. Our two favorite versions have been Peanut Butter Chocolate Chip and Toasted Coconut Cream. You and your kids can let your imaginations run wild as you discover other yummy creations. Happy summer!

To make popsicles: The popsicle molds should be at room temperature before assembling. Spray the inside of each mold with nonstick cooking spray. Set them aside.

Pop the molds into the freezer and freeze for 1 hour. After 1 hour, place a wooden stick inside each mold. Continue to freeze at least 7 hours before removing.

When ready to serve, run your sink until the water is very hot. Holding the mold, place the bottom portion under the hot water for about 20 to 30 seconds. After that, you should be able to grab the sticks and easily remove each popsicle. If they're not coming out easily, run the bottom of the mold under hot water a few seconds more. Remove, serve, and enjoy.

Peanut Butter Chocolate Chip Popsicles

This recipe makes ten popsicles.

INGREDIENTS

3 (5-ounce) containers vanilla-flavored Greek yogurt (I use Dannon Oikos single serve)

1½ cups creamy peanut butter

1 cup semi-sweet chocolate chips

10 wooden popsicle sticks

In a mixing bowl, combine the Greek yogurt and peanut butter with a spoon. Stir in the chocolate chips. Pour the mixture into the molds, leaving an inch on top.

Toasted Coconut Cream Popsicles

This recipe makes ten popsicles.

INGREDIENTS

3 (5-ounce) containers coconut-flavored Greek yogurt (I use Dannon Oikos single serve)

2 cups toasted coconut (see below)

10 wooden popsicle sticks

To toast the coconut, add sweetened, flaked coconut to a clean, dry skillet and toast for about 1 or 2 minutes over medium-high heat. Remove from the skillet and cool for 1 or 2 more minutes.

In a mixing bowl, combine the Greek yogurt and 1½ cups of toasted coconut with a spoon. Pour the mixture into the molds, leaving an inch on top. Lightly add the rest of the toasted coconut to the tops of each mold. (When you invert them, the toasted coconut will be at the bottom as pictured.)

☀ **Hint:** If you can't find coconut-flavored Greek yogurt, you can use vanilla Greek yogurt and add 1½ teaspoons of coconut extract to the mixing bowl when you're combining the yogurt with the toasted coconut. This is what I did!

LOVABLE

LUNCHES

I've said this a million times—lunch is hard for me! I'm really motivated to make breakfast, and I adore preparing dinner, but around noon I have no energy for making food (and cleaning up the mess). So in order to spark some enthusiasm, I've created several simple (and delicious!) recipes to make my midday a better day. Also, all of these recipes can be made with kids or tucked away in their lunchboxes for school. Lunch never looked so good!

Pizza Pasta Salad

Baked Turkey Corn Dog Bites

Lettuce Wrap Pasta Salad

Trees and Cheese Quesadillas

Crescent Roll Tacos

Bacon Marmalade Grilled Cheese Sandwich

Pizza Pasta Salad

You just can't go wrong with pasta for kids…hot or cold, they love it! It's so fun for the kids to toss these ingredients together. This salad is really simple, full of flavor, kid-tested, and mama-approved. A little pasta salad with the flavor of pizza? Well, you *really* can't go wrong with that! Win, win!

This recipe serves four portions for a light lunch or side dish.

INGREDIENTS

½ pound short-cut pasta (I use shells)

1 (8-ounce) can tomato sauce

1 tablespoon Italian seasoning

1½ cups pepperoni, chopped

1 cup cherry tomatoes

½ cup Parmesan cheese, grated

Bring a large pot of water to a boil, add the pasta, and cook until al dente (about 6 or 7 minutes).

After the pasta has cooked, immediately drain the hot water and then rinse the pasta under cold water to cool it off. Drain off all the cold water and set the pasta aside.

In a small bowl, combine the tomato sauce and Italian seasoning with a spoon. Pour this mixture over the pasta and then add the pepperoni, tomatoes, and cheese. Toss until everything is coated in tomato sauce. Cover and refrigerate the salad at least 2 hours before serving.

When you're ready to serve, remove from the fridge and garnish with a little more cheese.

Baked Turkey Corn Dog Bites

Every kid loves a hot dog for lunch, and these are even better than regular hot dogs! We buy our favorite turkey sausages, cut them into bite-sized pieces, and then dip them in cornbread batter. (Kids love the dipping part!) We bake them over a wire rack, and *bam!*…little baked corn dogs for lunch. You can make the plate a little more colorful—and nutritious—by adding some spinach leaves and orange slices. Such a simple lunch for your bunch.

This recipe makes about eight corn dog bites.

INGREDIENTS

1 (13-ounce) package precooked turkey sausage, cut into bite-sized pieces

1 (8-ounce) box corn muffin mix

1 egg

⅓ cup milk

Salt and pepper

Preheat the oven to 425 degrees.

Line a baking sheet with foil and then place your baking rack right on top. Spray the baking rack with Pam so nothing sticks. Set these aside.

In a small bowl, combine the corn muffin mix, egg, and milk with a fork. Stir in a nice pinch of both salt and pepper. Take each piece of turkey sausage and coat it in the corn muffin batter. Place each corn dog on the prepared baking rack. Once they're all lined up, pop them in the oven and bake about 10 minutes or until the corn dog bites are lightly browned. Remove them from the oven and serve immediately.

Lettuce Wrap Pasta Salad

I'm the pasta salad queen. During the summer, we often make a pasta salad and eat some of it several days in a row. We'll pack it in the cooler to take to the pool, eat it on the patio if we're home for lunch, or add it to our supper as a side dish. Pasta salads are the perfect blank canvas for everything but the kitchen sink, which is just what you want when you're in the kitchen with your kiddos. For this recipe, we took our favorite flavors from a lettuce wrap and turned it into a pasta salad. So good!

This recipe will serve four as a main course or six if you're having it as a side dish.

INGREDIENTS

1 pound short-cut pasta

1 garlic clove, finely chopped

½ cup hoisin sauce

3 tablespoons soy sauce

1 (8-ounce) can sliced water chestnuts, drained

1 cup raw cashews

1 red bell pepper, chopped

About 8 green onions, chopped

3 cups fresh spinach leaves, chopped into bite-sized pieces

Toasted sesame seeds to garnish

Bring a pot of water to boil over medium-high heat. Once the water is boiling, add the pasta and cook until just shy of al dente (about 4 minutes). Immediately drain the pasta water, rinse with cold water, and drain. Reserve your cold, cooked pasta.

Put the garlic in a small bowl and whisk in the hoisin and soy sauces. Set this aside.

Add the water chestnuts, cashews, bell pepper, onions, and spinach leaves to the pasta. Next, drizzle the sauce over the top and toss everything together.

To toast the sesame seeds, add a couple of tablespoons of seeds to a dry skillet and toast over medium-high heat for about a minute. Garnish the pasta with the toasted sesame seeds.

Cover and refrigerate at least an hour before serving.

I keep this in the fridge at least three days and munch on it as the days go by. If you want your cashews and sesame seeds to stay nice and crunchy, you can leave them out and garnish with them each day.

Hint: If you like your pasta salad a little "saucier," you can double the sauce ingredients.

One of my favorite tips for serving lunches to kiddos (especially young kiddos) is to have a picnic on the floor. I realized I was tired of cleaning up around our kitchen table between breakfast and dinner, so I started laying out a big beach towel, and we have a picnic-style lunch indoors. This way, after we're done eating, I just fold up the towel, shake it off over the trash, and the mess is cleaned up. Some of my best mom memories are shared lunches on the floor with my kids.

Trees and Cheese Quesadillas

I've discovered that if I call broccoli "trees," my kiddos will eat them up. I've also found that they'll eat anything I put inside a quesadilla. Thus, my Trees and Cheese Quesadillas are always a big hit! My kids love to sprinkle cheese on the "trees" in these tasty little favorites. We also like to put in some chopped green chilies for extra flavor (not heat), but if your kiddos wouldn't love that, leave them out!

This recipe makes eight quesadillas.

INGREDIENTS

4 flour tortillas

About 2 cups chopped broccoli florets

1 (4-ounce) can chopped green chilies

1 cup cheese (I use Gruyère), shredded

Preheat an indoor griddle or a big skillet to medium-high heat. Coat it lightly with cooking spray.

Lay out 2 flour tortillas. Place 1 cup of broccoli across each tortilla. Add a few tablespoons of green chilies and a sprinkle of cheese. Take the other two tortillas and place them on top of the broccoli mixture.

Place 1 quesadilla in the skillet. Brown it on both sides (about 4 minutes or so for each side). Once it's browned, remove it and slice it in half and then in half again (to give you four from each whole quesadilla). Repeat with the other quesadilla.

Crescent Roll Tacos

These little Crescent Roll Tacos are such a simple lunch…and simple is always good! Kids love to assemble these yummy guys and *mix and match* the ingredients. Not only are they easy to prepare, but they're great for using up your leftovers too. If you have leftover ground beef or turkey from the night before, just add it right in. You can also use leftover chicken. We also love that this little lunch is hearty enough to serve for dinner too.

This recipe makes eight little tacos.

INGREDIENTS

1 can crescent rolls

1 (15-ounce) can refried beans (you won't use all of it)

About ½ pound ground beef (leftovers are perfect!), browned and crumbly

2 tablespoons chili powder

About a cup of taco sauce or salsa

A sprinkle of cheese (optional)

Chopped green onions (optional)

Preheat the oven to 350 degrees.

Lightly spray a cookie sheet with cooking spray. Set it aside.

Roll out the crescent rolls into 8 triangles. Spoon a little bit of refried beans on the bottom half of each triangle. If your ground beef isn't already seasoned from the night before, toss it in the chili powder. Once it's been combined, spoon the ground beef mixture over the refried beans. Add a little drizzle of taco sauce to the top of the ground beef, followed by the cheese and green onions.

Roll each crescent roll so that the other half covers the half with the mixture on it. Place each crescent taco on the prepared baking sheet.

Bake about 8 minutes and then serve immediately.

Bacon Marmalade
Grilled Cheese Sandwich

Grilled cheese…a tried-and-true kid favorite. And to make it a *mom* favorite, try this new twist…
with candied jalapeños, orange marmalade, bacon, and spinach. Seriously…this sandwich is my
favorite—and my kiddos love it too. If you and your kids haven't cooked with candied jalapeños,
don't be scared! They have big flavor but aren't too hot. You really just need to make this!

This makes enough for one sandwich…multiply it out if you're making this for more people.

INGREDIENTS

2 pieces bread (I use a Jewish rye)

A slice of Cheddar and a slice of Gruyère
(I like to grate mine to make it melt more evenly)

2 pieces bacon, cooked crisp (I use turkey bacon)

6 or 8 candied jalapeños

A few fresh spinach leaves

Orange marmalade

Preheat your grill pan or a large skillet to medium-high. Lightly coat it with cooking spray.

Assemble your sandwich by first spreading marmalade on both slices of bread. Next assemble
the bread, spinach, cheese, bacon, and jalapeños and top with bread. Grill your sandwich until the
cheese is nice and melted (flipping it over halfway). If you want your sandwich to be really decadent,
spread a little butter on the outside of both pieces of bread before grilling.

Once the cheese is melted, slice and serve.

Need some fun lunchbox ideas? Mix it up!

- **I write notes on my kiddos' napkins** every single day (and draw a few little pictures too!).

- We **pop popcorn** for a little crunch.

- We **cut our sandwiches into shapes** that correspond with the season (hearts for Valentine's Day, pumpkins for Halloween, trees for Christmas...).

- I let them **make their own trail mix blend** in the bulk foods aisle of our grocery store, and then we bag it up for their snack at school. (They love having their own special concoction!)

- We sometimes **use Nutella or vanilla almond butter** for a little change on their PB&J sandwiches.

PIZZA, PASTA, AND OTHER POSSIBILITIES

At some point during the day, my kids always ask me what's for dinner. and nothing puts a bigger smile on their little faces then when I say either pizza or pasta. They are kid food all the way! I've become creative over the years and changed up the standard pizza and pasta recipes for a little more variety. Occasionally, I even marry the two. Talk about happy campers at dinner! When pizza and pasta combine, their whole world is made.

Pizza Boats
Baked Pizza Pasta Casserole
Spooky Spaghetti
Lemon Parm Pasta
Butternut Squash Mac and Cheese

Pizza Boats

This is my mother-in-law's recipe. She used to make pizza boats with my husband and his brother while they were growing up, and now we make them with our kids too. Anything "pizza" is always a huge hit with kids!

This recipe servers four.

INGREDIENTS

4 English muffins, split in half

1 pound ground beef (or ground turkey)

1 (8-ounce) can tomato paste

2 tablespoons Italian seasoning

¼ cup olives, finely chopped (optional)

A handful of sliced pepperoni (I use turkey)

2 cups mozzarella cheese, shredded

A handful of Parmesan cheese, grated (optional)

Preheat the oven to 350 degrees.

Place the English muffins on a baking sheet lined with foil (for easy cleanup). If you're using 4 English muffins, you will have 8 halves spread out on your baking sheet. Set these aside.

In a large skillet over medium-high heat, brown the ground beef. Once it's browned and crumbly, stir in the tomato paste and Italian seasoning (and chopped olives if you like). Reduce the heat to low.

Place a few slices of pepperoni on each English muffin and then spoon a little ground beef mixture across the top. Sprinkle on a little mozzarella and finish off with a bit of Parmesan if you like.

Place the baking sheet in your oven and bake about 10 minutes or until the cheese is nice and bubbly and melted.

Remove and serve immediately.

Baked Pizza Pasta Casserole

Pasta and pizza are kid favorites in our household. Probably in yours too! Always easy, always yummy, and always great for little helpers to join in. This simple supper is a pasta that tastes just like pizza. So family friendly!

This recipe servers four.

INGREDIENTS

1 pound pasta cooked to al dente (I use shells but you could use ziti, penne, or rigatoni)

1 pound ground beef (or ground chicken or turkey)

1 onion, chopped

2 cloves garlic, chopped

1 (10-ounce) can condensed tomato soup

1 (14-ounce) bottle pizza sauce

1 cup sliced pepperoni (I use turkey pepperoni but you can use what you love)

1 cup mozzarella cheese, shredded

1 cup panko (or your favorite breadcrumbs)

Extra virgin olive oil

Salt and pepper

Preheat the oven to 350 degrees.

Bring a large pot of water to a boil over medium-high heat. Add the pasta and cook until al dente (about 6 or 7 minutes).

Brown the ground beef with the onion and garlic and a drizzle of olive oil in a skillet over medium-high heat. Once the meat is browned and crumbly, sprinkle with a little salt and pepper, reduce heat to low, and stir in the tomato soup, pizza sauce, cooked noodles, and pepperoni.

At this point, if your skillet isn't oven-safe, transfer the mixture to an 8 x 8 baking dish.

Sprinkle the cheese and panko (or breadcrumbs) on top of the casserole, cover with foil, and bake 20 minutes. Remove the foil and bake another 5 minutes or until browned and bubbly.

Remove from the oven and serve.

Spooky Spaghetti

There's nothing like being in the kitchen with my kids during the holidays. We have so much fun making special food for each season. The recipes don't have to be complicated...you just need a little imagination and a lot of togetherness. We love making Spooky Spaghetti to serve before trick-or-treating begins...or really anytime during October. Of course, you can make any version of spaghetti and call it spooky...but why not make a real family-friendly variety in honor of this *spooktacular* day?

This recipe serves four.

INGREDIENTS

1 pound spaghetti or linguine noodles

1 pound ground beef

1 onion, chopped

3 garlic cloves, chopped

1½ tablespoons chili powder

1 (10-ounce) can Ro-Tel tomatoes

1 (8-ounce) can tomato sauce

1 (28-ounce) can peeled tomatoes (I use San Marzanos)

About 2 cups Cheddar cheese (I use a sharp white Cheddar), shredded

Torn basil leaves to garnish

Extra virgin olive oil

Salt and pepper

Bring a large pot of water to a boil, add the pasta, and cook until al dente (about 6 or 7 minutes).

Meanwhile, in a large skillet over medium-high heat, brown the ground beef in a drizzle of olive oil. Once the meat is browned and crumbly, add the onion and garlic along with a big pinch of salt and pepper. Once the onions are tender, sprinkle in the chili powder. Next, stir in the Ro-Tel tomatoes, tomato sauce, and peeled tomatoes. Reduce heat to low and simmer about 10 minutes. Stir often and break up the whole tomatoes with the back of your wooden spoon.

Once the pasta is cooked to al dente, drain the water off and add the hot pasta to the spaghetti sauce. Stir in the shredded cheese (reserving just a little bit for a garnish). Portion out the pasta among the plates and garnish with a little more cheese and some torn basil.

I learned a long time ago that oftentimes, it's the name of what kids are eating that will inspire tasting more than anything else. Can't get your kids to eat spaghetti? Tell them it's spooky spaghetti and see if their interest isn't piqued. Quirky names and funny recipes can almost always get kiddos to try their supper.

Lemon Parm Pasta

In our house, pasta suppers aren't just for summer or winter. My kiddos love pasta year-round, so during the warm months, we swap out heavy sauces for lighter ingredients. The kids like tossing in whatever ingredients we have on hand...but lemon is a definite *must* here! This yummy dish can be a vegetarian entrée, and it's also a great side to grilled summer foods, like chicken, pork, fish, or shrimp. Oh, we just love our Lemon Parm Pasta! Simple, simple, simple and yummy, yummy, yummy.

This recipe serves four people as an entrée and six to eight as a side dish.

INGREDIENTS

1 pound pasta (I use whole wheat but you can use what you like)

3 to 4 tablespoons extra virgin olive oil

Zest and juice of 2 lemons (about 2 tablespoons of zest and ½ cup or so of juice)

½ cup grated Parmesan cheese (plus more for garnish)

½ cup chopped parsley (plus more for garnish)

Salt and pepper

Bring a large pot of water to boil over medium-high heat. Add the pasta and cook to al dente (about 6 or 7 minutes).

Drain the water from the pasta and immediately add other ingredients. Toss in the olive oil, lemon zest, lemon juice, Parmesan cheese, parsley, and a pinch of salt and pepper. Serve immediately with a little more zest, cheese, and parsley to garnish.

☀ **Hint:** We like to use linguine for this supper, but it really works with any variety of pasta shapes.

Butternut Squash Mac and Cheese

I'm always looking for ways to add butternut squash or pumpkin to our family's fall dishes. I love the flavor, and I also love the extra boost of veggies—with all those good vitamins—for my kiddos. The other night, we made this Butternut Squash Mac and Cheese for dinner along with some brisket, and it was a huge hit!

This recipe makes enough for four supper portions or a side dish for six.

INGREDIENTS

1 pound short-cut pasta (I use shells)

Extra virgin olive oil

1 shallot (or red onion), diced

2 tablespoons flour

1 cup milk

1 (10-ounce) package thawed and pureed butternut squash

1 cup Cheddar cheese, shredded

½ cup Parmesan cheese, grated (plus a little extra for garnish)

About 4 tablespoons fresh thyme, roughly chopped

Salt and pepper

Bring a large pot of water to a boil over medium-high heat and add the pasta. Cook until al dente (about 6 or 7 minutes).

Meanwhile, in a large saucepan over medium-high heat, sauté the shallot in about 2 tablespoons of olive oil and a nice pinch of salt and pepper for about 3 minutes or until nice and tender. Add another drizzle of olive oil. Next, whisk in the flour and cook about 1 minute. Then whisk in the milk. Whisk everything together about a minute before whisking in the pureed squash. Continue whisking over medium-high heat until the sauce thickens (it takes a couple of minutes). Once the sauce is thick enough to coat your spoon, whisk in the Cheddar and Parmesan cheese along with the thyme.

Drain the water from the cooked pasta and pour the squash mixture on top of the pasta. Serve immediately and garnish with a little extra Parmesan and thyme.

Note: If your sauce starts to thicken a bit too much, just whisk in a bit more milk until it reaches a nice mac and cheese consistency.

A few notes on this recipe:

- This would make a great vegetarian pasta supper as well as a side dish.

- You can roast, peel, dice, and puree your own whole butternut squash, or you can use a 10-ounce bag of frozen butternut. My grocery store offers the frozen squash already pureed and also cubed. Whichever you select, just thaw it in the microwave before adding it in. If you want to make the cubed squash nice and smooth, zip it through your blender or food processor after it's thawed. Easy!

DINNER WITHOUT THE WHINE

I don't know about you, but nothing can ruin a family dinner more than a whiny kid. "Why do we have to eat that?" And "how many more bites?" are two of the most dreaded questions this mama sometimes hears. I like to think in advance and eliminate as much of the whine as I can. My solution? Kid-friendly recipes everyone in the house will enjoy. Sometimes it's all about presentation with kiddos. (See Meatloaf Muffins!)

Popcorn Chili

Hot Dog Soup

Pesto Meatballs

Sloppy Joe Pot Pies

Cheeseburger Meatball Sliders

Meatloaf Muffins

Jalapeño Peach Chicken

Sausage and Shells

Cajun Shrimp Pasta

Crispy Shrimp Tacos

Tex-Mex Ravioli Bake

Popcorn Chili

Sometimes all it takes to get kids to try something new is to put a silly spin on it. You know how adults put crushed tortilla chips or crackers on their chili? Well, why not popcorn? Crunchy, salty… and perfect when piled on a bowl of chili. And bonus—your kids will think it's super fun and totally crazy to eat popcorn on their dinner…before you know it, they're eating chili! I make this version with ground beef, but ground turkey would work too. And the best part? This is a slow-cooker supper!

This recipe serves four.

INGREDIENTS

1 pound ground beef
1 onion, chopped
3 tablespoons chili powder
1 (14-ounce) can diced tomatoes
1 (8-ounce) can tomato sauce
1 (6-ounce) can tomato paste

1 (15-ounce) can red kidney beans, rinsed and drained
Extra virgin olive oil
Salt and pepper
Shredded Cheddar cheese to garnish (optional)
Popped popcorn to garnish

In a large skillet over medium-high heat, brown the ground beef in a drizzle of olive oil until it's browned and crumbly. Add the onion and a pinch of salt and pepper. Sauté about 3 minutes and then stir in the chili powder.

Transfer this mixture to your slow cooker and then add the diced tomato, tomato sauce, tomato paste, and kidney beans. Cover and cook on low for 6 to 8 hours or on high for 3 to 4 hours.

Remove the lid when you're ready to serve and ladle the chili into bowls. Garnish with the Cheddar cheese and popcorn.

Hot Dog Soup

Kids love hot dogs, right? And pasta? So if you put them together in a bowl of soup, they might end up loving soup too! We don't use real hot dogs (although you could if you wanted to!). We like to slice up a turkey kielbasa. Kids love to help by adding the ingredients and stirring the soup. And they love the name of this warm, yummy bowl of goodness!

This recipe serves four.

INGREDIENTS

1 pound elbow noodles (I use whole wheat)

1 pound kielbasa sausage, chopped (I use a precooked turkey sausage)

1 onion, chopped

1 (15-ounce) can black beans, rinsed and drained

1 (10-ounce) can Ro-Tel tomatoes

1 (6-ounce) can tomato paste

About a cup of chicken stock

Extra virgin olive oil

Salt and pepper

Bring a large pot of water to a boil and add the pasta. Cook until al dente (about 6 or 7 minutes). Remove from heat, drain the water, and set the pasta aside.

Meanwhile, in a stock pot over medium-high heat, sauté the chopped sausage and onion in a drizzle of olive oil and a pinch of salt and pepper until the onions are tender (about 5 minutes). Add the beans, Ro-Tel tomatoes, tomato paste, and stock. Reduce heat to low and simmer about 10 minutes.

When you're ready to serve, add the cooked pasta to the stock pot and stir. Ladle the soup into dishes and enjoy.

Pesto Meatballs

Meatball night is a big deal at our house. The kids love the taste of meatballs, and I love them because I can hide all sorts of veggies inside. Sometimes we cook up a side of pasta for the kiddos, and my husband and I eat our meatballs with a big side salad. You could totally prepare this spaghetti-and-meatball style or use these guys as an appetizer. I make ten large meatballs with this recipe, but you and your kids can make them any size. Make them mini, make them large...just make them!

This recipe yields about 10 large meatballs.

INGREDIENTS

1 pound ground beef

3 cloves garlic, chopped

1 cup panko (or your favorite breadcrumbs)

½ cup Parmesan cheese, grated

1 box frozen spinach, thawed and with all excess water squeezed out

½ cup pesto (I use store-bought, but you could make your own)

2 eggs, beaten

2 splashes milk

Salt and pepper

Extra virgin olive oil

Spaghetti sauce for dipping or drizzling on top (optional)

Preheat the oven to 425 degrees.

In a medium bowl, combine the ground beef, garlic, panko, cheese, spinach, pesto, eggs, and milk. Add just a pinch of salt and pepper. Roll the mixture into balls (I make mine golf-ball size) and place them on a lightly greased baking sheet (I always line with foil for easy cleanup!). Drizzle olive oil over the meatballs. Roast in the oven about 20 minutes or until brown.

Remove from the oven and toss with your favorite pasta, or serve on toothpicks as appetizers, or simply enjoy with a big side salad.

Sloppy Joe Pot Pies

What do you get when you take two favorite comfort foods and marry them together? Pot pie plus sloppy joe equals perfection! My kids can't get enough of this recipe. They're really big fans of sloppy joes...but when they get to add a biscuit on top? *Huge* fans! This is that super-quick weeknight recipe every family needs. So simple, and you can totally swap out the ground beef for ground turkey or chicken.

This recipe makes four really big individual pot pies or one large pot pie that will yield four large portions.

INGREDIENTS

1 pound ground beef
1 onion, chopped
1 (10-ounce) can condensed tomato soup (I use Campbell's)
2 tablespoons Worcestershire sauce
1 (16-ounce) can refrigerated biscuit dough (I use Pillsbury Grands)
Extra virgin olive oil
Salt and pepper

Preheat the oven to 375 degrees.

Grease (I use Pam) either an 8 x 8 baking dish or 4 individual oven-safe bowls. Set them aside.

In a large skillet over medium-high heat, sauté the ground beef in a drizzle of olive oil. Once the meat is browned and crumbly, add the chopped onion and a liberal pinch of both salt and pepper. Sauté just a few more minutes or until the onions are tender. Stir in the tomato soup and Worcestershire sauce. Pour the ground beef mixture into your prepared baking dish and then top with the uncooked biscuits. If you're using individual serving dishes, top each bowl with two biscuits.

Place the serving dish(es) in the oven and bake about 10 minutes or until the tops of the biscuits are browned.

Remove from the oven and serve immediately.

Now, the bottoms of your biscuits won't brown because they're resting on the sloppy joe mixture. We love it this way, but if you want your entire biscuit cooked through, you'll need to cook them separately (perhaps while the mixture is simmering on the stove) and then just top your sloppy joe mixture with them and immediately serve. Either way, delish!

One night, I took two of our family's favorite recipes and married them together: sloppy joes and pot pies. Two favorites, one new dinner, and six happy Shulls!

Cheeseburger Meatball Sliders

Hamburgers are always a kid favorite, and these fun little meatball sliders are even better! My kiddos love stirring up the meatball mixtures, which is oh-so-simple to make, and piling on their favorite condiments. Part meatball, part cheeseburger, all served on slider rolls and sure to satisfy your hungry family!

This recipe serves four (and makes about 12 meatballs).

INGREDIENTS

1 pound ground beef

2 eggs, lightly beaten

1 tablespoon steak seasoning

1 cup breadcrumbs or panko

1½ cups Cheddar cheese, shredded

Slider buns

Chopped red onion, mustard, ketchup, and/or relish to garnish

Preheat the oven to 425 degrees.

Spread foil across a cookie sheet (for easy cleanup) and then lightly coat with cooking spray. Set it aside.

In a mixing bowl, combine the ground beef, eggs, steak seasoning, breadcrumbs, and Cheddar. Divide the mixture into golf-ball-sized portions and roll into balls. Place each meatball on the prepared cookie sheet.

Place the tray of meatballs in the oven and roast for about 18 to 20 minutes.

Remove the meatballs from the oven and add them to the slider buns. Top them with your favorite condiments. We like mustard and ketchup, chopped red onion, and relish on our sliders.

Meatloaf Muffins

Meatloaf is hands-down my husband's favorite meal. To make it a little more kid-friendly, I turn my standard meatloaf into little muffins. The kids get involved by putting paper muffin liners into the tins or greasing the muffin tin. (Paper muffin liners are fun because they come in such colorful patterns!) The same great recipe in a fun new presentation that kids will adore!

This recipe serves four and makes about 10 to 12 muffins.

INGREDIENTS

1 pound ground beef

1 cup breadcrumbs or panko

2 eggs, beaten

1 onion, chopped

Salt

5 tablespoons Worcestershire sauce

1 (8-ounce) can tomato sauce

1 cup ketchup

⅔ cup brown sugar

1 teaspoon mustard

Preheat the oven to 350 degrees.

Grease (I use Pam) a standard 12-cup muffin tin. Set it aside.

Combine the ground beef, breadcrumbs, eggs, onion, salt, tomato sauce, and 3 tablespoons of the Worcestershire sauce in a large mixing bowl. Divide the mixture between the muffin cups and bake 25 minutes.

Meanwhile, combine the ketchup, brown sugar, mustard, and remaining 2 tablespoons of Worcestershire sauce in a bowl. After 25 minutes, spoon the mixture on top of each muffin and pop them back in the oven for an additional 5 minutes.

Remove from the oven and serve immediately.

Jalapeño Peach Chicken

I'm kind of jalapeño-obsessed. I have a yummy jalapeño peach jam in my fridge that I use on breakfast sandwiches, so I decided to take that flavor combo and turn it into a supper. This is such a good weeknight meal because you can make chicken for the whole family, and the kids can add either the jalapeño relish or their own condiments, like ketchup or BBQ sauce. Easy!

This recipe serves four.

INGREDIENTS

4 boneless chicken breast halves

2 eggs, lightly beaten

2 cups all-purpose flour

Salt and pepper

1½ cups peach preserves

1 jalapeño, seeded and chopped (you can also use jarred deli jalapeños)

About 6 green onions, chopped

Preheat the oven to 400 degrees.

Line a baking sheet with foil and lightly spray with Pam (for easy cleanup).

In a shallow dish, lightly beat the two eggs (I use a pie plate for this). In a second shallow dish, combine the flour with a generous pinch of salt and pepper.

Dip each piece of chicken first in the flour, then in the beaten egg, and then back in flour. Place the coated pieces on the baking sheet and repeat with the rest of your chicken.

Bake the chicken about 20 minutes or until it's nice and crispy and the juices run clear when pierced with a fork. To make the jalapeño peach relish, combine the peach preserves with the jalapeños and green onions (reserving a few pieces for garnish) in a bowl. Keep refrigerated until ready to serve.

Remove the chicken from the oven and garnish with the jalapeño peach relish.

Sausage and Shells

My kids love pasta, and they love sliced sausage. (They call this dish "hot dog pasta.") So this is the perfect supper for our family! We use turkey sausage links chopped into pieces, but you can absolutely use pork. We also use a mild sausage and then add the red pepper flakes (depending on how spicy the kiddos want it), but you can also skip the red pepper flakes and just use a spicy sausage. *Mix and match* it…the ideal kid-friendly pasta supper!

This recipe serves four.

INGREDIENTS

1 pound shell pasta

1 pound sausage links, chopped into pieces

1 onion, chopped

3 or 4 garlic cloves, chopped

1 (14-ounce) can diced tomatoes (or use Ro-Tel tomatoes for extra spice!)

1 (8-ounce) can tomato sauce

1 tablespoon Italian seasoning

1 or 2 teaspoons crushed red pepper flakes (optional)

3 tablespoons half-and-half, cream, or milk (whatever you have on hand)

Parmesan cheese, grated, to garnish

Extra virgin olive oil

Bring a large pot of water to a boil over medium-high heat. Add the pasta and cook it until al dente (about 6 or 7 minutes).

Meanwhile, in a large skillet over medium-high heat, sauté the sausage, onion, and garlic in a drizzle of olive oil. Once the onion is tender (about 5 minutes), add the tomatoes, tomato sauce, Italian seasoning, and red pepper flakes. Reduce heat to low and simmer another 5 to 10 minutes.

Once the pasta is cooked, drain the water off and add the hot pasta to your tomato sauce mixture. Stir in the cream. Remove from heat and ladle into bowls with Parmesan cheese as your garnish.

Cajun Shrimp Pasta

My kids are shrimp-obsessed. And noodle-obsessed. So when we make noodles and shrimp together in one meal, they are super pumped! This little supper can be on your table in minutes. Really and truly, what takes the longest in making this dinner is waiting for the water to boil.

And don't be scared about the heat level in this dish. You control the heat! This recipe is flavorful but mild enough for kiddos. If you'd like more heat, just add more seasoning. Like every perfect family recipe, it's up to you!

This entree serves four.

INGREDIENTS

1 pound pasta (we use linguine)

1 onion, chopped

3 cloves garlic, chopped

1 red bell pepper, chopped

1 tablespoon Cajun seasoning
(or you can use more)

1½ pounds shrimp, peeled and deveined

1 big splash heavy cream, whipping cream, half-and-half, or milk

About two handfuls basil, torn

Extra virgin olive oil

Salt and pepper

Bring a large pot of water to a boil over medium-high heat. Add the pasta and cook until al dente (about 6 or 7 minutes).

Meanwhile, in a large skillet over medium-high heat, sauté the chopped onion in a tablespoon or so of olive oil for about 4 or 5 minutes and then add a big pinch of salt and pepper. Add the garlic and red bell pepper and sauté another minute or two. Next, add the shrimp and Cajun seasoning. Cook about 3 or 4 minutes.

Remove about a cup of the water from your pasta pot and set it aside. Drain the rest of the water off the pasta and add the hot pasta to the shrimp skillet. Add your reserved cup of water and toss everything together (the starchy cooking water will help everything come together). Finally, stir in a big splash of cream or milk and then add the basil.

Remove from heat and serve. One big skillet of perfect pasta.

☀ **Hint:** You can find Cajun seasoning blends on the spice aisle of your grocery store.

Crispy Shrimp Tacos

My kids are obsessed with anything shrimp, so these fun tacos are a great spin on a weeknight supper. Bonus—my kids can help me bread the shrimp, which always excites them!

This recipe serves four.

INGREDIENTS

1½ pounds shrimp, peeled and deveined

2 cups plain breadcrumbs

4 tablespoons chili powder

Salt and pepper

1 red onion, chopped

1 (15-ounce) can black beans, drained and rinsed

1 pint cherry tomatoes, halved

Guacamole

1 lemon

1 (8-ounce) container sour cream

8 flour tortillas, warmed

Preheat the oven to 400 degrees.

Line a baking sheet with foil (for easy cleanup) and lightly spray it with Pam. Set it aside.

In a bowl, combine the breadcrumbs, 3 tablespoons of chili powder, and a big pinch of salt and pepper. Toss the shrimp in the breadcrumb mixture. Place the shrimp on the baking sheet (trying not to overlap them).

Bake the shrimp about 10 to 12 minutes or until they are nice and crispy.

Meanwhile, assemble your toppings. To make the sour cream extra special, stir the remaining tablespoon of chili powder into it.

To assemble the tacos, spread guacamole down the center of each tortilla. Next, add crispy shrimp, chopped red onion, some black beans, a few cherry tomatoes, a squeeze of lemon juice, and a dollop of sour cream.

Tex-Mex Ravioli Bake

Easy cleanup is important when you're cooking with kids! We like to make this recipe when my husband is out of town. We use cheese ravioli, which makes the meal vegetarian, but you could most definitely use beef or chicken ravioli instead. The bottom line is...this supper is so simple! Simple to make and simple to clean up. Score one for mom!

This recipe serves four.

INGREDIENTS

2 (9-ounce) packages cheese ravioli

10 to 12 green onions, chopped

1 (10-ounce) can Ro-Tel tomatoes

1 (15-ounce) can black beans, drained and rinsed

1 (8-ounce) can tomato sauce

1 cup frozen corn

1 tablespoon chili powder (or a 1-ounce packet taco seasoning)

1 cup Cheddar cheese, shredded

Preheat the oven to 425 degrees.

Grease (I use Pam) a pie plate or an 8 x 8 baking dish. Set it aside.

Bring a large pot of water to a boil over medium-high heat. Add the ravioli and cook it until al dente (about 4 minutes). Drain the water and reserve the ravioli.

Meanwhile, in a mixing bowl, combine the green onions (reserve a few for garnish), Ro-Tel tomatoes, black beans, tomato sauce, corn, and chili powder.

Pour the cooked ravioli across the bottom of your prepared baking dish and then top it with the black bean mixture. Sprinkle cheese on top of everything and bake it for 15 to 20 minutes or until the casserole is nice and bubbly and the cheese has melted.

Remove from the oven and serve.

It's good to throw out a meat-free meal from time to time. My Tex-Mex Ravioli is so hearty and full of flavor, your family will never miss the meat.

SWEETS
FOR MY
SWEETIES

Sometimes we like to end our meals with a little something sweet. A special dessert is all it takes to turn a boring old Tuesday into something special. Plus, your kids can practically make all of these recipes themselves from start to finish. A few simple ingredients and a couple of steps is all it takes to make sweets for your sweeties.

Easiest Peanut Butter Cookies

Dessert Pizza

Peanut Butter Rice Krispies Treats

S'mores Pie

Soda Pop-sicles

Lemon Ice Box Pie with a Golden Oreo Crust

Waffle Sundaes

Easiest Peanut Butter Cookies

Nothing says kids like cookies…and especially peanut butter cookies! Every mama needs an easy peanut butter cookie recipe in her repertoire. And this one is perfect…just four ingredients. Kids can practice using the electric mixer (low and slow!), and they love pressing down the tops of the unbaked cookies with a fork. Classic. Simple. Yummy.

This recipe makes one dozen cookies.

INGREDIENTS

1 cup creamy peanut butter

1 cup sugar

1 egg

1 teaspoon vanilla

Preheat the oven to 350 degrees.

Lightly coat a cookie sheet with cooking spray and set it aside.

In a mixing bowl, beat with an electric mixer all four ingredients. Once they are combined, spoon the batter onto cookie sheet in 12 little balls. Use a fork to lightly press down the top of each ball.

Pop the cookie sheet in the oven and bake 9 to 10 minutes.

Remove from oven and enjoy.

Dessert Pizza

My kids asked to make a dessert pizza…and since it was getting close to Easter, I asked them if they wanted to make a jelly bean version. Needless to say, they were all over that suggestion! You can make this little pizza any way you like. It's super yummy with sliced fruit like kiwi, strawberries, blueberries, and banana. You can also top it with chocolate chips or candy, a little cinnamon, a bit of Nutella…go nuts (hey, you can add nuts too!). This is just about the best dessert you can make with kids.

INGREDIENTS

1 tube sugar cookie dough or homemade sugar cookie dough

4 ounces cream cheese, softened (half a block)

2 cups powdered sugar

1 teaspoon vanilla extract

1 tablespoon milk

Jelly beans, other candies, or fruit to decorate

Preheat the oven to 350 degrees.

Lightly spray a baking sheet with cooking spray.

On your clean kitchen counter, roll out the sugar cookie dough into a big circle. Our circle was about 10 inches in diameter.

Place the dough on your prepared baking sheet and bake about 14 or 15 minutes or until lightly browned. Remove the giant sugar cookie from the oven and let it cool completely on the counter before decorating.

In a mixing bowl, beat with an electric mixer the cream cheese, powdered sugar, vanilla, and milk. Spread the mixture on top of the cooled "pizza" crust. Decorate with the jelly beans or whatever you like!

Peanut Butter Rice Krispies Treats

My grandmother's Peanut Butter Rice Krispies Treats were the first thing I ever learned to make on my own. I was eight the first time I could make them, and I still make them to this day. So of course this is a recipe I wanted to share with my kids! My son kept telling me he could make them by himself too, so when we had time in the kitchen…just the two of us…I let him "make" them. I did the stove part since he's only five, but he did the rest!

INGREDIENTS

1 cup sugar

1 cup light corn syrup

1 cup creamy peanut butter

6 cups Rice Krispies cereal

In a small saucepan over medium-high heat, bring the sugar and corn syrup up to a boil, stirring continuously. Once it's at a low boil, remove from heat and stir in the peanut butter. Pour the peanut butter mixture over the cereal in a large mixing bowl. Combine quickly until the cereal is covered and then spread it out in a well-greased (I use Pam) 8 x 8 baking dish. Cool at least 10 minutes before cutting into squares.

Smith measured the six cups of cereal by himself, he measured the sugar and put it in the saucepan, then he measured the Karo syrup. Then I brought everything to a boil before removing it from the heat and having him stir in the peanut butter. Finally, Smith poured everything into the baking dish and flattened it into bars. He was so proud of himself!

S'mores Pie

I adore anything s'mores. So this simple little pie was totally my happiness. And yep, my kids kind of loved it too. And loved *making* it…all those tasty ingredients for them to sample! They helped me assemble it…super quick…and then it was ready and waiting for us at dessert time. A little graham cracker, a lot of chocolate, and marshmallow too. Have s'more!

This recipe makes one nine-inch pie.

INGREDIENTS

1 (3-ounce) box instant chocolate pudding

1 cup milk

1 cup whipped topping (I use Cool Whip), thawed slightly

1 cup chocolate chips (plus more for garnish)

2 cups mini marshmallows (plus more for garnish)

1 prepared graham cracker crust

In a large mixing bowl, whisk the dry chocolate pudding mix and milk for about two minutes. Whisk in the Cool Whip until just combined. Stir in the chocolate chips and mini marshmallows (reserving some for garnish).

Pour the mixture into the pie crust and refrigerate at least 4 hours or up to 2 days.

Remove the pie from the fridge, garnish it with a few more chocolate chips and mini marshmallows, and serve.

Soda Pop-sicles

Yep, we're popsicle crazy around here! One hot day we got the inspiration to take three bottles of soda...and turn them into yummy frozen treats! Grab your favorite soda and some fun add-ins, and you're good to go. This is like a science experiment and an art project all in one. We love to combine cola with cherries, orange soda with white chocolate chips (tastes like a Dreamsicle!), and vanilla cream soda with chocolate chips (my favorite). We also want to try root beer and butterscotch chips, and lemon-lime soda with lemon zest. Easy. Fun. Fast. Frozen. The perfect summer treat!

This recipe makes ten popsicles.

INGREDIENTS

2 (12-ounce) bottles of your favorite soda

10 wooden popsicle sticks

A few little add-ins (we added 3 cherries per pop-sicle or about a tablespoon of chocolate chips)

The popsicle molds should be at room temperature before assembling. Spray the inside of each mold with nonstick cooking spray.

Slowly pour the soda into the molds, leaving an inch on top. Carefully drop your add-ins into the molds.

Pop the molds into the freezer and freeze for 1 hour. After 1 hour, place the wooden sticks inside each mold. Continue to freeze at least 7 hours before removing.

When you're ready to serve, run the bottom part of the mold under very hot water for about 20 to 30 seconds. After that, you should be able to grab the sticks and easily remove each popsicle. If they're not coming out easily, run the bottom of the mold under hot water a few seconds more.

Remove, serve, and enjoy.

Lemon Ice Box Pie with a Golden Oreo Crust

Looking for the perfect simple dessert to make with your kids? There's nothing simpler than an ice box pie. All you need to do is mix, pour, freeze, and enjoy. My kids and I loved making (and eating!) this pie. They especially loved making the crust out of Oreos. It's best to make this one day in advance and then, when you're ready to serve it, pop it out of the freezer, slice, and enjoy. It's a little bite of sunshine in every single bite!

This makes one nine-inch pie.

INGREDIENTS

About 1½ cups crushed Golden Oreos (about 12)
6 tablespoons melted butter
1 (8-ounce) package cream cheese, softened

1 (14-ounce) can sweetened condensed milk
Zest and juice of 2 lemons (about 4 tablespoons of juice and 3 or 4 of zest)

Lightly spray a pie plate with cooking spray and set it aside.

For the crust: In your food processor, pulse the crushed Oreos until they resemble a fine powder. Add the melted butter and pulse until it's all combined. Remove the mixture and pat it inside the pie plate. Make sure you pat it up the sides as well as across the bottom. Freeze about 1 hour before filling.

For the filling: With an electric mixer, beat together the cream cheese, condensed milk, lemon zest, and lemon juice until they are combined. Pour the lemon mixture into the pie shell (after it's been in the freezer an hour). Cover the pie and freeze it at least 4 hours (up to 24).

When you're ready to serve the pie, remove it from freezer and slice and serve.

Waffle Sundaes

When I was 12 years old, my grandparents took me to Maui. Every morning, my grandfather let me order a waffle for breakfast topped with ice cream, fudge, whipped cream, and sprinkles. When I came home from that trip and told my mom, she said, "So you basically ate an ice cream sundae every morning for breakfast?"

Yes, Mom. Yes I did.

Now that I'm a mom, I'm using the same fun method but letting my kids eat it for dessert instead of breakfast. All you do is assemble it—which means kids can make this recipe all by themselves!

INGREDIENTS

Pancake or waffle mix and the ingredients to prepare them

Vanilla ice cream

Whipped cream

Hot fudge

Sprinkles

Prepare your waffle mix and whip up some delicious waffles for the base. After your waffles are finished, top them with your favorite ice cream, whipped cream, fudge, and sprinkles.

HOORAY

FOR

HOLIDAYS

I'm a big believer in celebrating every holiday, big or small. From Valentine's Day to Christmas, I get absolutely giddy making seasonal holiday recipes with my kids. Without a doubt, these are the recipes we look forward to the most and talk about long after they're gone. Holiday recipes create memories and define childhood moments. They are something not to be missed.

Valentine's Day	Cherry Chip Cookies
St. Paddy's Day	Lucky Charms Treats
Easter	Macaroons
Independence Day	Red, White, and Blueberry Pie
Halloween	Monster Mix
Thanksgiving	Mini Pumpkin Pies
Christmas	Hot Chocolate Cupcakes with Peppermint Buttercream Frosting

Valentine's Day—Cherry Chip Cookies

What's better than making valentines? Making valentines you can *eat!* This super simple, super quick recipe combines two favorites—chocolate and cherries—and is the perfect way to say "I love you." These are awesome to tuck in school lunches or to serve at a Valentine's Day party. Remember, Valentine's Day is all about love…and we love being a family. So make these cookies with your sweeties and celebrate!

This recipe makes about two dozen cookies.

INGREDIENTS

1 box white cake mix
1 (3-ounce) box cherry gelatin
2 eggs

½ cup vegetable oil
1 cup chocolate chips

Preheat the oven to 350 degrees.

In a mixing bowl, combine the cake mix, gelatin, eggs, and vegetable oil with a spatula until everything is combined. Stir in the chocolate chips.

Drop the dough onto a greased cookie sheet by the tablespoonful and bake about 8 to 10 minutes.

Remove the cookies from the oven and let them cool on the baking sheet about 5 minutes before transferring them to a wire rack to finish cooling.

St. Paddy's Day—Lucky Charms Treats

Call me crazy, but I really enjoy St. Patrick's Day! As a mom, it's especially fun because my kids and I can make the whole day green and silly. In honor of St. Patrick's Day and all that Irish blood I have in me, we make Rice Krispie treats, but instead of Rice Krispies cereal…we use Lucky Charms! These are delicious, and we have the best time making them together. Simple and fast… only three ingredients required. And you can *mix and match* these in a million different ways!

INGREDIENTS

3 tablespoons butter

5 cups marshmallows

6 cups Lucky Charms cereal

Melt the butter in a microwavable bowl (about 30 seconds or so). Add the marshmallows and coat them with the melted butter. Microwave another minute and a half or so until the marshmallows are melted. Remove from the microwave and immediately add the cereal. Mix well and then spread in a greased 8 x 8 baking dish (use a 9 x 13 baking dish for thinner treats). Spray a spatula with Pam and press down the cereal so it will stay put in the baking dish.

Let the bars cool in the baking dish about 20 minutes before slicing them into squares.

Easter—Macaroons

We love celebrating the most important holiday of them all, Easter, with my yummy macaroons. It is always a very special day of the year for us as we remember that Christ is risen. My family typically makes a lot of desserts with either carrots or coconut for our Easter celebration. These easy Easter macaroons are a perfect fit!

This recipe makes about 18 macaroons.

INGREDIENTS

5½ cups sweetened coconut flakes

⅓ cup all-purpose flour

½ teaspoon salt

1 (14-ounce) can sweetened condensed milk

1 teaspoon vanilla

8 ounces vanilla almond bark

Easter sprinkles (pastel colors)

Preheat your oven to 350 degrees.

Spray your cookie sheet with Pam or line it with parchment paper. Set it aside.

In a mixing bowl, combine the coconut flakes and flour with a wooden spoon. Stir in the salt, milk, and vanilla.

Drop the dough onto your parchment paper (about two tablespoons per macaroon).

Bake 15 to 20 minutes or until the macaroons are lightly browned and toasted.

Remove from the oven to cool for 1 minute while you're preparing the almond bark.

Microwave the almond bark, stirring every 45 seconds until smooth. Drizzle the melted almond bark over each macaroon and then go back and quickly add sprinkles on top (the almond bark will set quickly).

Serve either warm or at room temperature. Store in an airtight container on the counter.

☀ **Hint:** Almond bark is sold on the chocolate chip aisle and typically comes in a 24-ounce package (with 12 2-ounce squares). You only need 4 squares. You can use a vanilla candy coating too… sold in a similar package. Either will work just fine.

Change up your sprinkles and you can have any kind of macaroon you want…Fourth of July Macaroons, Valentine's Day Macaroons, Halloween Macaroons, Christmas Macaroons…you get the idea.

Independence Day—Red, White, and Blueberry Pie

For our favorite summer holiday, we always like a dessert with a little red, white, and blue...or in this case, blueberry. An easy, no-bake pudding pie is almost simple enough for kids to make on their own! And if your kids are like my kids, they'll each want to be the one to pulse the crumbs together for the crust. From beginning to end, this recipe is perfect for summertime kids in the kitchen!

This recipe makes one pie.

INGREDIENTS

About 1½ cups crushed Nilla Wafers (about 20 or so)

6 tablespoons melted butter

1 (3-ounce) box instant vanilla pudding

1 cup milk

1 (21-ounce) can strawberry pie filling

Whipped cream or Cool Whip

Fresh blueberries to garnish

For the crust: Pulse the crumbled Nilla Wafers in your food processor until they are fine. Add the melted butter and pulse until it's all combined. Remove the mixture and pat it inside the pie plate. Make sure you pat it up the sides as well as across the bottom. Freeze it for about an hour before filling.

For the filling: In a large mixing bowl, whisk together the dry vanilla pudding mix and milk for about 2 minutes. Whisk in the strawberry pie filling until they are just combined.

Remove the crust from the freezer and pour in the strawberry pudding mixture.

Cover and refrigerate the pie at least 4 hours and up to 2 days.

Remove the pie from the fridge and garnish with a little whipped cream and some fresh blueberries.

Halloween—Monster Mix

Mixes are about the most kid-friendly recipes out there! My kiddos absolutely love making mixes, and this one is no exception. It has so many goodies…Apple Cinnamon Cheerios, Vanilla Chex, marshmallows, and Halloween candy. I call it Monster Mix (because *hello?* I love alliteration!), but one of my kids calls it Bat Mix because he says that's so much scarier. Monster Mix, Bat Mix, Spooky Mix, Halloween Mix…just make the mix. Your little pumpkins will love it!

This recipe makes a ton! You'll get about 12 cups of mix.

INGREDIENTS

4 cups Apple Cinnamon Cheerios

4 cups Vanilla Chex cereal

8 ounces white candy coating or almond bark

1 (9-ounce) bag fall-colored M&M's

1 (9-ounce) bag candy corn

A big handful of mellowcreme pumpkins

2 cups mini marshmallows

Halloween sprinkles

Lay wax paper on your kitchen counters to pour your Monster Mix on.

Combine the Cheerios and Chex in a large mixing bowl.

Melt the candy coating in a microwavable bowl, stirring every 45 seconds. Once it's melted, quickly pour it over your cereal mixture and toss. Working quickly, add the M&M's, candy corn, mellowcreme pumpkins, mini marshmallows, and sprinkles, and then pour the mixture over the wax paper to dry (about 10 minutes). Once it's dried, store in an airtight container.

This is a really cute Halloween treat for teachers, neighbors, friends, or family. Just tie it up in a little clear bag and add an orange or black ribbon.

Thanksgiving—Mini Pumpkin Pies

Nothing says fall and Thanksgiving to me like pumpkins. Every year we look forward to pulling out our pumpkin decorations and making our house cozy. Pumpkins just make us happy…so, so happy! And pumpkin treats? Even happier! My little turkeys love these Mini Pumpkin Pies. So cute. So cozy. So easy. This fall, you and your kiddos owe it to yourselves to make them. Of course you do!

This method makes 2 dozen mini pies.

INGREDIENTS

1 (16-ounce) tube refrigerated sugar cookie dough (or make your own from scratch)

1 (3-ounce) box instant pumpkin pudding mix (available during the fall)

2 cups milk

Whipped cream and cinnamon to garnish

Preheat the oven to 350 degrees.

Grease (I use Pam) a 24-cup mini muffin tin.

Slice a piece of cookie dough off the tube and press it inside each muffin cup to form a crust.

Bake the cookie crusts about 10 minutes or until lightly browned.

Remove from the oven and allow to cool completely. Remove each crust from the pan before filling.

In a mixing bowl, whisk together the pudding mix and milk about 5 minutes or until thickened. Add a dollop of pudding mix to each cooled cookie crust. Refrigerate the mini pies at least 30 minutes to firm them up.

Remove the mini pies from the fridge and garnish with a little whipped cream and a sprinkle of cinnamon.

Serve and enjoy!

Christmas—Hot Chocolate Cupcakes with Peppermint Buttercream Frosting

Early in the Christmas season, we love to make these yummy, festive, and simple cupcakes. They combine all the kid favorites of the season—hot chocolate, peppermint, and Christmas candy. Really, what could be better? Cupcakes are so fun for kiddos to make…the mixing and the pouring and the frosting and the decorating. They're the perfect little party treat for all of your merry and bright nights!

This recipe makes 2 dozen cupcakes.

INGREDIENTS

1 box chocolate cake mix

3 tablespoons instant hot chocolate powder

½ cup vegetable oil

1¼ cups water

4 eggs

1 (8-ounce) package cream cheese, softened

3 cups powdered sugar

1 or 2 tablespoons milk

2 teaspoons peppermint extract

Red food coloring

Peppermint crunch, candy cane marshmallows, peppermint M&M's, or candy cane Kisses to garnish

Preheat the oven to 350 degrees.

Line 2 12-cup muffin tins with cupcake liners.

Combine the cake mix, hot chocolate powder, oil, water, and eggs in a mixing bowl with an electric mixer.

Pour the batter into the prepared muffin tins and bake 16 to 18 minutes or until a toothpick inserted comes out clean.

Let the cupcakes rest on the counter in the pan 5 minutes before removing them to a wire rack to finish cooling.

To make the frosting, beat the cream cheese, powdered sugar, and milk with an electric mixer until smooth. Add more powdered sugar if your frosting is too thin and more milk if it's too thick. Beat in the peppermint extract and a few drops of red food coloring until they are incorporated.

Frost the cooled cupcakes with the peppermint cream cheese frosting and garnish with your favorite Christmas candy.

One of my kids' favorite things to do for a holiday is gift someone a baked goodie. We love to make it, bake it, bag it, and share it with our neighbors, friends, and family. Sharing food with the ones you love (especially over a holiday) is such a sweet and personal lesson to learn early in life.

Acknowledgments

Well, this book wouldn't have been created if not for my four precious children and my wonderful husband. Kensington, Smith, Ashby, and Madeley...words cannot express how grateful I am to be your mom. The Lord has blessed me so much with you four, and I know that when I look back on my life, times spent in the kitchen with you will be among my most cherished memories. And to my sweet husband, Andrew, who is the best dad and husband we could ask for. We love you so much.

Thank you to the wonderful people at Harvest House who make my dreams come true book after book. Your hard work, love, encouragement, and support are so appreciated. I am blessed to know so many amazing and talented people. Thank you all so much.

Thank you to my amazing agent, Ruth Samsel, who told me from the beginning that I needed to do a book about kids in the kitchen. You have such a big heart for family...and for me. Thank you.

And, of course, thank you so much to everyone who visits my blog every day. Your love, support, encouragement, and enthusiasm over the last ten years of blogging have impacted my life more than you'll ever know. I am humbled, grateful, and so appreciative of this little community of online friends. God bless each and every one of you.

My life is nothing without Christ Jesus. I'm thankful each and every day for the love, grace, mercy, and forgiveness He gives me.

SHAY SHULL is the author of the *Mix and Match Mama* blog, *Mix-and-Match Mama Eats, Mix-and-Match Meal Planner,* and *Mix-and-Match Cakes*. She writes about motherhood, adoption, world travel, holidays, organization, and, of course, yummy food. Passionate about coffee, traveling the world with her family, and Red Sox baseball, her greatest love is Christ. Shay lives in McKinney, Texas, with her husband, Andrew, and their four kids: Kensington, Smith, Ashby, and Madeley.

Connect with Shay on social media as **@mixandmatchmama**.

Use **#kidsinthekitchen** to share your special time cooking with your kiddos.

Recipe Index

Meals Your Whole Family Will Love.

The pressure of planning and preparing meals from one day to the next can become stressful. Shay Shull, the Mix and Match Mama, has found simple solutions for making quick and tasty dishes that will satisfy your whole family and make your life so much easier.

Discover more than 200 crazy good go-to breakfast, dinner, and dessert recipes for every holiday, season, and month of the year, as well as a helpful Tips and Tricks section featuring "Baking Essentials" and "Grocery Staples."

Let Shay show you how to spend less time in the kitchen and more time making memories as you enjoy home-cooked meals your entire family will love.

Turn Shay's tastiest recipes into easy weekly meal plans with the ***Mix-and-Match Meal Planner***, with bonus content such as helpful shopping and pantry essentials lists, tips and tricks for streamlining your cooking, and dozens of great ideas to help you make dinner fun for the whole family.

Get all of Shay's 101 tasty cake recipes in one helpful collection. ***Mix-and-Match Cakes*** will help you discover the simple secret to delicious, "wow-worthy" cakes that will have your family and friends begging for your recipe. You'll be inspired to make every day a little sweeter.

DINNER? DESSERT? DONE.
* IT'S THAT SIMPLE! *

To learn more about Harvest House books and
to read sample chapters, visit our website:

www.harvesthousepublishers.com

HARVEST HOUSE PUBLISHERS
EUGENE, OREGON